The Constitution *of the* Confederate States of America

REPRINTED BY

Wake Forest, NC
www.scuppernongpress.com

The Constitution of the Confederate States of America

Edited by Frank B. Powell, III

©2021 The Scuppernong Press

First Printing

The Scuppernong Press
PO Box 1724
Wake Forest, NC 27588
www.scuppernongpress.com

Cover and book design by Frank B. Powell, III

All rights reserved

Printed in the United States of America

No part of this book may be reproduced or transmitted in any form or by any means, electronic or mechanical, including photocopying, recording, or by any information and storage and retrieval system, without written permission from the editor and/or publisher.

International Standard Book Number
ISBN 978-1-942806-41-7

Contents

Introduction 1

Preamble 3

Article I 4

Article II 17

Article III 22

Article IV 24

Article V 26

Article VI 26

Article VII 28

The constitution of the Confederate States of America was very similar to the United States of America Constitution. And why shouldn't it be? After all, a Southerner, James Madison, was the chief architect of the US Constitution and it was adopted by their forefathers. This was the main reason the states of the South declared their independence and seceded to form their own government. The northern states and the Federal government had strayed from the constitution adopted by their forefathers.

The Confederate Constitution has a different feeling right from the start when it adds some language to correct what was not included in the US Constitution. State sovereignty and independence and invoking God's favor, guidance and blessings are incorporated in the Confederate Constitution preamble.

Unlike the United States Constitution, the Confederate Constitution does not allow the importation of slaves from Africa or any other foreign country except the United States. No, this does not mean the South was fighting to uphold slavery as some modern day *faux* historians would claim.

Another main difference is voting by foreign born people is not allowed in any election for any office, civil or political, State or federal.

The president was elected to one, six-year term and could not be reelected. However, the vice president could be reelected. In addition, the president did have line item veto power on appropriation bills.

Most of the Bill of Rights in the United States Constitution was incorporated into the Confederate Constitution.

There are other small adjustments and tweaks throughout the document to correct things Southerners felt were in error with the original document and to balance power between the states and the federal government.

— Frank B. Powell, III, editor

The Constitution *of the* Confederate States of America

Preamble

WE, the People of the Confederate States, each State acting in its sovereign and independent character, in order to form a permanent Federal government, establish Justice, insure domestic tranquility, and secure the Blessings of Liberty to ourselves and our Posterity, invoking the favor and guidance of Almighty God, do ordain and establish this Constitution for the Confederate States of America.

ARTICLE I

SECTION I

All legislative Powers herein delegated, shall be vested in a Congress of the Confederate States, which shall consist of a Senate and House of Representatives.

SECTION II

1) The House of Representatives shall be composed of Members chosen every second Year by the People of the several States, and the Electors in each State shall be citizens of the Confederate States, and have the Qualifications requisite for Electors of the most numerous Branch of the State Legislature; but no person of foreign birth, and not a citizen of the Confederate States, shall be allowed to vote for any officer, civil or political, State or Federal.

2) No Person shall be a Representative who shall not have attained to the Age of twenty-five Years, and be a citizen of the Confederate States, and who shall not, when elected, be an Inhabitant of that State in which he shall be chosen.

3) Representatives and direct Taxes shall be apportioned among the several States which may be included within this Confederacy, according to their respective Numbers, which shall be determined by adding to the whole Number of free Persons, including those bound to Service for a Term of Years, and excluding Indians not taxed, three-fifths of all slaves. The actual Enumeration shall be made within three Years after the first Meeting of the Congress of the Confederate States, and within every subsequent Term of ten Years, in such Manner as they shall by Law direct. The Number of Representatives shall not exceed one for every fifty Thousand, but each State shall have at Least one Representative; and until such enumeration shall be made, the State of South Carolina shall be entitled to choose six, the State of Georgia ten, the State of Alabama nine, the State of Florida two, the State of Mississippi seven, the State of Louisiana six, and the State of Texas six.

4) When vacancies happen in the Representation from any State, the Executive Authority thereof shall issue Writs of Election to fill such Vacancies.

5) The House of Representatives shall choose their Speaker and other Officers; and shall have the sole Power of Impeachment; except that any judicial or other federal officer resident and acting solely within the limits of any State, may be impeached by a vote of two-thirds of both branches of the Legislature thereof.

SECTION III

1) The Senate of the Confederate States shall be composed of two Senators from each State, chosen by the Legislature thereof, for six Years, at the regular session next immediately preceding the commencement of the term of service; and each Senator shall have one Vote.

2) Immediately after they shall be assembled in Consequence of the first Election, they shall be divided as equally as may be into three Classes. The Seats of the Senators of the first Class shall be vacated at the Expiration of the second Year, of the second Class at the Expiration of the fourth Year, and of the third Class at the Expiration of the sixth Year, so that one-third may be chosen every second Year; and if Vacancies happen by Resignation, or otherwise, during the Recess of the Legislature of any State, the Executive thereof may make temporary Appointments until the next Meeting of the Legislature, which shall then fill such Vacancies.

3) No Person shall be a Senator who shall not have attained to the Age of thirty Years, and be a citizen of the Confederate States, and who shall not, when elected, be an Inhabitant of that State for which he shall be chosen.

4) The Vice President of the Confederate States shall be President of the Senate, but shall have no Vote, unless they be equally divided.

5) The Senate shall choose their other Officers, and also a President *pro tempore*, in the Absence of the Vice President, or when he shall exercise the Office of President of the United States.

6) The Senate shall have the sole Power to try all Impeachments. When sitting for that Purpose, they

shall be on Oath or Affirmation. When the President of the Confederate States is tried, the Chief Justice shall preside: And no Person shall be convicted without the Concurrence of two-thirds of the Members present.

7) Judgment in Cases of Impeachment shall not extend further than to removal from Office, and Disqualification to hold and enjoy any Office of honour, Trust or Profit under the Confederate States; but the Party convicted shall nevertheless be liable and subject to Indictment, Trial, Judgment and Punishment, according to Law.

SECTION IV

1) The Times, Places and Manner of holding Elections for Senators and Representatives, shall be prescribed in each State by the Legislature thereof, subject to the provisions of this Constitution; but the Congress may at any time by Law make or alter such Regulations, except as to the times and places of choosing Senators.

2) The Congress shall assemble at least once in every Year, and such Meeting shall be on the first Monday in December, unless they shall by Law appoint a different Day.

SECTION V

1) Each House shall be the Judge of the Elections, Returns and Qualifications of its own Members, and a Majority of each shall constitute a Quorum to do Business; but a smaller Number may adjourn from day to day, and may be authorized to compel the Attendance of absent Members, in such Manner, and under such Penalties as each House may provide.

2) Each House may determine the Rules of its Proceedings, punish its Members for disorderly Behaviour, and, with the Concurrence of two-thirds of the whole number expel a Member.

3) Each House shall keep a Journal of its Proceedings, and from time to time publish the same, excepting such Parts as may in their Judgment require Secrecy; and the Yeas and Nays of the Members of either House on any question shall, at the Desire of one-fifth of those Present, be entered on the Journal

4) Neither House, during the Session of Congress, shall, without the Consent of the other, adjourn for more than three days, nor to any other Place than that in which the two Houses shall be sitting.

SECTION VI

1) The Senators and Representatives shall receive a Compensation for their Services, to be ascertained by Law, and paid out of the Treasury of the Confederate States. They shall in all Cases, except Treason and Breach of the Peace, be privileged from Arrest during their Attendance at the Session of their respective Houses, and in going to and returning from the same; and for any Speech or Debate in either House, they shall not be questioned in any other Place.

2) No Senator or Representative shall, during the Time for which he was elected, be appointed to any civil Office under the Authority of the Confederate States, which shall have been created, or the Emoluments whereof shall have been increased during such time; and no Person holding any Office under the Confederate States, shall be a Member of

either House during his Continuance in Office. But Congress may, by law, grant to the principal officers in each of the executive departments a seat upon the floor of either House, with the privilege of discussing any measures appertaining to his department.

SECTION VII

1) All Bills for raising Revenue shall originate in the House of Representatives; but the Senate may propose or concur with Amendments as on other Bills.

2) Every Bill which shall have passed both Houses, shall, before it becomes a Law, be presented to the President of the Confederate States; If he approves he shall sign it, but if not he shall return it, with his Objections to that House in which it shall have originated, who shall enter the Objections at large on their Journal, and proceed to reconsider it. If after such Reconsideration two-thirds of that House shall agree to pass the Bill, it shall be sent, together with the Objections, to the other House, by which it shall likewise be reconsidered, and if approved by two-thirds of that House, it shall become a Law. But in all such Cases the Votes of both Houses shall be determined by Yeas and Nays, and the Names of the Persons voting for and against the Bill shall be entered on the Journal of each House respectively. If any Bill shall not be returned by the President within ten Days (Sundays excepted) after it shall have been presented to him, the Same shall be a law, in like Manner as if he had signed it, unless the Congress by their Adjournment prevent its return, in which Case it shall not be a Law. The President may approve any appropriation and disapprove any

other appropriation in the same bill. In such case he shall, in signing the bill, designate the appropriation disapproved, and shall return a copy of such appropriation, with his objections, to the House in which the bill shall have originated; and the same proceedings shall then be had as in case of other bills disapproved by the President.

3) Every Order, Resolution, or Vote to which the Concurrence of [the Senate and House of Representatives] both Houses may be necessary shall be presented to the President of the Confederate States; and before the Same shall take Effect, shall be approved by him, or being disapproved by him, [shall] may be re-passed by two-thirds of [the Senate and House of Representatives] both Houses, according to the Rules and Limitations prescribed in the Case of a Bill.

SECTION VIII

The Congress shall have Power —

1) To lay and collect Taxes, Duties, Imposts and Excises, for revenue necessary to pay the Debts [and], provide for the common Defence, and carry on the government of the Confederate States; but no bounties shall be granted from the treasury, nor shall any duties, or taxes, or importation from foreign nations be laid to promote or foster any branch of industry; and all Duties, Imposts and Excises shall be uniform throughout the Confederate States;

2) To borrow Money on the credit of the Confederate States;

3) To regulate Commerce with foreign Nations, and among the several States, and with the Indian Tribes; but neither this, nor any other

clause contained in this Constitution, shall ever be construed to delegate the power to Congress to appropriate money for any internal improvement intended to facilitate commerce; except for the purpose of furnishing lights, beacons, and buoys, and other aids to navigation upon the coasts, and the improvement of harbors, and the removing of obstructions in river navigation; in all such cases such duties shall be laid on the navigation facilitated thereby, as may be necessary to pay the costs and expenses thereof;

4) To establish a uniform Rule of Naturalization, and uniform Laws on the subject of Bankruptcies throughout the Confederate States; but no law of Congress shall discharge any debt contracted before the passage of the same;

5) To coin Money, regulate the Value thereof, and of foreign Coin, and fix the Standard of Weights and Measures;

6) To provide for the Punishment of counterfeiting the Securities and current Coin of the Confederate States;

7) To establish Post Offices and post routes; but the expenses of the Post office Department, after the first day of March, in the year of our Lord eighteen hundred and sixty-three, shall be paid out of its own revenues;

8) To promote the progress of Science and useful Arts, by securing for limited Times to Authors and Inventors the exclusive Right to their respective Writings and Discoveries;

9) To constitute Tribunals inferior to the supreme Court;

10) To define and punish Piracies and Felonies

committed on the high Seas, and Offenses against the Law of Nations;

11) To declare War, grant Letters of Marque and Reprisal, and make Rules concerning Captures on Land and Water;

12) To raise and support Armies, but no Appropriation of Money to that Use shall be for a longer Term than two Years;

13) To provide and maintain a Navy;

14) To make Rules for the Government and Regulation of the land and naval Forces;

15) To provide for calling forth the Militia to execute the Laws of the Confederate States, suppress Insurrections and repel Invasions;

16) To provide for organizing, arming, and disciplining the Militia and for governing such Part of them as may be employed in the Service of the Confederate States, reserving to the States respectively, the Appointment of the Officers, and the Authority of training the Militia according to the Discipline prescribed by Congress;

17) To exercise exclusive Legislation in all Cases whatsoever, over such District (not exceeding ten miles square) as may, by Cession of particular States, and the Acceptance of Congress, become the Seat of the Government of the Confederate States, and to exercise like Authority over all Places purchased by the Consent of the Legislature of the State in which the Same shall be, for the Erection of Forts, Magazines, Arsenals, Dock-Yards, and other needful Buildings; — And

18) To make all Laws which shall be necessary and proper for carrying into Execution the foregoing Powers, and all other Powers vested by this

Constitution in the Government of the Confederate States or in any Department or Officer thereof.

SECTION IX

1) The importation of negroes of the African race from any foreign country other than the slaveholding States or territories of the United States of America, is hereby forbidden; and Congress is required to pass such laws as shall effectually prevent the same.

2) Congress shall also have power to prohibit the introduction of slaves from any State not a member of, or territory not belonging to, this Confederacy.

3) The Privilege of the Writ of *Habeas Corpus* shall not be suspended, unless when in Cases of Rebellion or Invasion the public safety may require it.

4) No Bill of Attainder or *ex post facto* Law, or law denying or impairing the right of property in negro slaves, shall be passed.

5) No Capitation, or other direct, Tax shall be laid, unless in Proportion to the Census or Enumeration herein before directed to be taken.

6) No Tax or Duty shall be laid on Articles exported from any State, except by a vote of two-thirds of both Houses.

7) No Preference shall be given by any Regulation of Commerce or Revenue to the Ports of one State over those of another.

8) No Money shall be drawn from the Treasury, but in Consequence of Appropriations made by Law; and a regular Statement and Account of the Receipts and Expenditures of all public Money shall be published from time to time.

9) Congress shall appropriate no money from the Treasury except by a vote of two-thirds of

both Houses, taken by yeas and nays, unless it be asked and estimated for by some one of the heads of departments and submitted to Congress by the President; or for the purpose of paying its own expenses and contingencies; or for the payment of claims against the Confederate States, the justice of which shall have been officially declared by a tribunal for the investigation of claims against the Government, which it is hereby made the duty of Congress to establish.

10) All bills appropriating money shall specify in Federal currency the exact amount of each appropriation and the purposes for which it is made; and Congress shall grant no extra compensation to any public contractor, officer, agent or servant, after such contract shall have been made or such service rendered.

11) No Title of Nobility shall be granted by the Confederate States; and no Person holding any Office of Profit or Trust under them, shall, without the Consent of the Congress, accept of any present, Emolument, Office, or Title, of any kind whatever, from any King, Prince or foreign State.

12) Congress shall make no law respecting an establishment of religion, or prohibiting the free exercise thereof; or abridging the freedom of speech, or of the press; or the right of the people peaceably to assemble, and to petition the Government for a redress of grievances.

13) A well-regulated Militia, being necessary to the security of a free State, the right of the people to keep and bear Arms shall not be infringed.

14) No Soldier shall, in time of peace, be quartered in any house, without the consent of the

Owner, nor in time of war, but in a manner to be prescribed by law.

15) The right of the people to be secure in their persons, houses, papers, and effects, against unreasonable searches and seizures, shall not be violated, and no Warrants shall issue, but upon probable cause, supported by Oath or affirmation, and particularly describing the place to be searched, and the persons or things to be seized.

16) No person shall be held to answer for a capital, or otherwise infamous crime, unless on a presentment or indictment of a Grand Jury, except in cases arising in the land or naval forces, or in the Militia, when in actual service in time of War or public danger; nor shall any person be subject for the same offence to be twice put in jeopardy of life or limb; nor shall be compelled in any Criminal Case to be a witness against himself, nor be deprived of life, liberty or property without due process of law; nor shall private property be taken for public use, without just compensation.

17) In all criminal prosecutions, the accused shall enjoy the right to a speedy and public trial, by an impartial jury of the State and district wherein the crime shall have been committed, which district shall have been previously ascertained by law, and to be informed of the nature and cause of the accusation; to be confronted with the witnesses against him; to have Compulsory process for obtaining Witnesses in his favour, and to have the Assistance of Counsel for his defense.

18) In Suits at common law, where the value in controversy shall exceed twenty dollars, the right of trial by jury shall be preserved, and no fact tried by

a jury shall be otherwise reexamined in any Court of the Confederate States, than according to the rules of the common law.

19) Excessive bail shall not be required, nor excessive fines imposed, nor cruel and unusual punishments inflicted.

20) Every law or resolution having the force of law, shall relate to but one subject, and that shall be expressed in the title.

SECTION X

1) No State shall enter into any Treaty, Alliance, or Confederation; grant Letters of Marque and Reprisal; coin Money; make any Thing but gold and silver Coin a Tender in Payment of Debts; pass any Bill of Attainder, or ex post facto Law, or Law impairing the Obligation of Contracts, or grant any Title of Nobility.

2) No State shall, without the consent of the Congress, lay any Imposts or Duties on Imports or Exports, except what may be absolutely necessary for executing its inspection Laws: and the net Produce of all Duties and Imposts, laid by any State on Imports or Exports, shall be for the Use of the Treasury of the Confederate States; and all such Laws shall be subject to the Revision and Control of the Congress.

3) No State shall, without the Consent of Congress, lay any Duty of Tonnage, except on seagoing vessels, for the improvement of its rivers and harbors navigated by the said vessels; but such duties shall not conflict with any treaties of the Confederate States with foreign nations; and any surplus of revenue thus derived shall, after making such improvement, be paid into the common treasury; nor

shall any State keep Troops, or Ships of War in time of Peace, enter into any Agreement or Compact with another State, or with a foreign Power, or engage in War, unless actually invaded, or in such imminent Danger as will not admit of Delay. But when any river divides or flows through two or more States, they may enter into compacts with each other to improve the navigation thereof.

ARTICLE II

SECTION I

1) The executive power shall be vested in a President of the Confederate States of America. He and the Vice President shall hold their offices for the term of six years; but the President shall not be re-eligible. The President and Vice President shall be elected as follows:

2) Each State shall appoint in such Manner as the Legislature thereof may direct, a Number of Electors, equal to the whole Number of Senators and Representatives to which the State may be entitled in the Congress; but no Senator or Representative, or Person holding an Office of Trust or Profit under the Confederate States, shall be appointed an Elector.

3) The Electors shall meet in their respective States, and vote by ballot for President and Vice President, one of whom, at least, shall not be an inhabitant of the same State with themselves; they shall name in their ballots the person voted for as President, and in distinct ballots the person voted for as Vice President, and they shall make distinct lists of all persons voted for as President, and of all persons voted for as Vice President, and of the number of votes for each, which lists they shall sign and certify, and transmit sealed to the seat of the government of the [United] Confederate States, directed to the President of the Senate; — The President of the Senate shall, in presence of the Senate and House of Representatives, open all the certificates and the votes shall then be counted; — The person having the greatest number of votes for President shall be the President, if such number be a majority of

the whole number of Electors appointed; and if no person have such majority, then from the persons having the highest numbers not exceeding three on the list of those voted for as President, the House of Representatives shall choose immediately, by ballot, the President. But in choosing the President, the votes shall be taken by States, the representation from each State having one vote; a quorum for this purpose shall consist of a member or members from two-thirds of the States, and a majority of all the States shall be necessary to a choice. And if the House of Representatives shall not choose a President whenever the right of choice shall devolve upon them, before the fourth day of March next following, then the Vice President shall act as President, as in the case of the death or other constitutional disability of the President.

4) The person having the greatest number of votes as Vice President shall be the Vice President, if such number be a majority of the whole number of Electors appointed, and if no person have a majority, then from the two highest numbers on the list the Senate shall choose the Vice President; a quorum for the purpose shall consist of two-thirds of the whole number of Senators, and a majority of the whole number shall be necessary to a choice.

5) But no person constitutionally ineligible to the office of President shall be eligible to that of Vice President of the Confederate States.

6) The Congress may determine the Time of choosing the Electors, and the Day on which they shall give their Votes; which Day shall be the same throughout the Confederate States.

7) No Person except a natural born Citizen of the

Confederate States, or a citizen thereof, at the time of the Adoption of this Constitution, or a citizen thereof born in the United States prior to the 20th of December, 1860, shall be eligible to the Office of President; neither shall any Person be eligible to that Office who shall not have attained to the Age of thirty-five Years, and been fourteen Years a Resident within the limits of the Confederate States, as they may exist at the time of his election.

8) In Case of the Removal of the President from Office, or of his Death, Resignation, or Inability to discharge the Powers and Duties of the said Office, the same shall devolve on the Vice President, and the Congress may by Law provide for the Case of Removal, Death, Resignation, or Inability, both of the President and Vice President, declaring what Officer shall then act as President, and such Officer shall act accordingly, until the Disability be removed, or a President shall be elected.

9) The President shall, at stated Times, receive for his Services, a Compensation, which shall neither be increased nor diminished during the Period for which he shall have been elected, and he shall not receive within that Period any other Emolument from the [United] Confederate States or any of them.

10) Before he enters on the Execution of his Office, he shall take the following Oath or Affirmation: —

"I do solemnly swear (or affirm) that I will faithfully execute the Office of President of the Confederate States, and will to the best of my Ability, preserve, protect and defend the Constitution thereof."

SECTION II

1) The President shall be Commander-in-Chief of the Army and Navy of the Confederate States, and of the Militia of the several States, when called into the actual Service of the Confederate States; he may require the Opinion, in writing, of the principal Officer in each of the executive Departments, upon any Subject relating to the Duties of their respective Offices, and he shall have Power to grant Reprieves and Pardons for Offenses against the Confederate States, except in Cases of Impeachment.

2) He shall have Power, by and with the Advice and Consent of the Senate, to make Treaties, provided two-thirds of the Senators present concur; and he shall nominate, and by and with the Advice and Consent of the Senate, shall appoint Ambassadors, other public Ministers and Consuls, Judges of the supreme Court, and all other Officers of the Confederate States, whose Appointments are not herein otherwise provided for, and which shall be established by Law: but the Congress may by Law vest the Appointment of such inferior Officers, as they think proper, in the President alone, in the Courts of Law, or in the Heads of Departments.

3) The principal officer in each of the executive departments, and all persons connected with the diplomatic service, may be removed from office at the pleasure of the President. All other civil officers of the executive department may be removed at any time by the President, or other appointing power, when their services are unnecessary, or for dishonesty, incapacity, inefficiency, misconduct, or neglect of duty; and when so removed, the removal shall be

reported to the Senate, together with the reasons therefore.

4) The President shall have Power to fill all Vacancies that may happen during the Recess of the Senate, by granting Commissions which shall expire at the End of their next Session.

SECTION III

The President shall from time to time give to the Congress Information of the State of the Confederacy, and recommend to their Consideration such Measures as he shall judge necessary and expedient; he may, on extraordinary Occasions, convene both Houses, or either of them, and in Case of Disagreement between them, with Respect to the Time of Adjournment, he may adjourn them to such Time as he shall think proper; he shall receive Ambassadors and other public Ministers; he shall take Care that the Laws be faithfully executed, and shall Commission all the officers of the Confederate States,

SECTION IV

The President, Vice President and all civil Officers of the Confederate States, shall be removed from Office on Impeachment for, and Conviction of, Treason, Bribery, or other high Crimes and Misdemeanors.

ARTICLE III

SECTION I

The judicial Power of the Confederate States shall be vested in one Superior Court, and in such inferior Courts as the Congress may from time to time ordain and establish. The Judges, both of the supreme and inferior Courts, shall hold their Offices during good Behavior, and shall, at stated Times, receive for their Services a Compensation, which shall not be diminished during their Continuance in Office.

SECTION II

1) The judicial Power shall extend to all cases, arising under this Constitution, in law and equity, the Laws of the Confederate States, and Treaties made, or which shall be made, under their Authority;- to all Cases affecting Ambassadors, other public Ministers, and Consuls; — to all Cases of admiralty and maritime Jurisdiction; — to Controversies to which the Confederate States shall be a Party; — to Controversies between two or more States; — between a State and Citizens of another State where the State is plaintiff ; — between Citizens claiming lands under grants of different' States, — and between a State, or the Citizens thereof, and foreign States, Citizens or Subjects; but no State shall be sued by a citizen or subject of any foreign State.

2) In all Cases affecting Ambassadors, other public Ministers and Consuls, and those in which a State shall be Party, the supreme Court shall have original Jurisdiction. In all the other Cases before

mentioned, the supreme Court shall have appellate Jurisdiction, both as to Law and Fact, with such Exceptions, and under such Regulations as the Congress shall make.

3) The Trial of all Crimes, except in Cases of Impeachment, shall be by Jury; and such Trial shall be held in the State where the said Crime[s] shall have been committed; but when not committed within any State, the Trial shall be at such Place or Places as the Congress may by Law have directed.

SECTION III

1) Treason against the Confederate States shall consist only in levying War against them, or in adhering to their Enemies, giving them Aid and Comfort. No Person shall be convicted of Treason unless on the Testimony of two Witnesses to the same overt Act, or on Confession in open Court.

2) The Congress shall have Power to declare the Punishment of Treason, but no Attainder of Treason shall work Corruption of Blood, or Forfeiture except during the Life of the Person attained.

ARTICLE IV

SECTION I

Full Faith and Credit shall be given in each State to the public Acts, Records, and judicial Proceedings of every other State. And the Congress may by general Laws prescribe the Manner in which such Acts, Records and Proceedings shall be proved, and the Effect thereof.

SECTION II

1) The Citizens of each State shall be entitled to all Privileges and Immunities of Citizens in the several States, and shall have the right of transit and sojourn in any State of this Confederacy, with their slaves and other property; and the right of property in such slaves shall not be impaired.

2) A Person charged in any State with Treason, Felony, or other Crime, who shall flee from Justice, and be found in another State, shall on Demand of the executive Authority of the State from which he fled, be delivered up, to be removed to the State having Jurisdiction of the Crime.

3) No slave or Person held to Service or Labour in [one State] any State or Territory of the Confederate Slates under the Laws thereof, escaping or unlawfully carried into another, shall, in Consequence of any Law or Regulation therein, be discharged from such Service or Labour, but shall be delivered up on Claim of the Party to whom such slave belongs, or to whom such Service or Labour may be due.

SECTION III

1) Other States may be admitted into this

Confederacy by a vote of two-thirds of the whole House of Representatives and two-thirds of the Senate, the Senate voting by States; but no new State shall be formed or erected within the Jurisdiction of any other State; nor any State be formed by the Junction of two or more States, or Parts of States, without the Consent of the Legislatures of the States concerned as well as of the Congress.

2) The Congress shall have Power to dispose of and make all needful Rules and Regulations [respecting the Territory or other Property belonging to the United States; and nothing in this Constitution shall be so construed as to Prejudice any Claims of the United States, or of any particular State] concerning the property of the Confederate States, including the lands thereof.

3) The Confederate States may acquire new territory, and Congress shall have power to legislate and provide governments for the inhabitants of all territory belonging to the Confederate States lying without the limits of the several States, and may permit them, at such times and in such manner as it may by law provide, to form States to be admitted into the Confederacy. In all such territory the institution of negro slavery as it now exists in the Confederate States shall be recognized and protected by Congress and by the territorial government, and the inhabitants of the several Confederate States and territories shall have the right to take to such territory any slaves lawfully held by them in any of the States or Territories of the Confederate States.

4) The Confederate States shall guarantee to every State that now is, or hereafter may become, a member of this Confederacy, a Republican Form of

Government, and shall protect each of them against Invasion; and on Application of the Legislature, or of the Executive (when the Legislature is not in session) against domestic Violence.

ARTICLE V

Upon the demand of any three States, legally assembled in their several Conventions, the Congress shall summon a Convention of all the States, to take into consideration such amendments to the Constitution as the said States shall concur in suggesting at the time when the said demand is made; and should any of the proposed amendments to the Constitution be agreed on by the said Convention — voting by States — and the same be ratified by the Legislatures of two-thirds of the several States, or by Conventions in two-thirds thereof — as the one or the other mode of ratification may be proposed by the general Convention — they shall henceforward form a part of this Constitution. But no State shall, without its consent, be deprived of its equal representation in the Senate.

ARTICLE VI

1) The Government established by this Constitution is the successor of the Provisional Government of the Confederate States of America, and all laws passed by the latter shall continue in force until the same shall be repealed or modified; and all the officers appointed by the same shall remain in office until their successors are appointed and qualified or the offices abolished.

2) All Debts contracted and Engagements entered into, before the Adoption of this Constitution, shall be as valid against the Confederate States under this Constitution, as under the Provisional Government.

3) This Constitution and the Laws of the Confederate States made in Pursuance thereof; and all Treaties made, or which shall be made, under the authority of the Confederate States, shall be the supreme Law of the Land; and the Judges in every State shall be bound thereby, anything in the Constitution or Laws of any State to the Contrary notwithstanding.

4) The Senators and Representatives before mentioned, and the Members of the several State Legislatures, and all executive and judicial Officers, both of the Confederate States and of the several States, shall be bound by Oath or Affirmation, to support this Constitution; but no religious Test shall ever be required as a Qualification to any Office or public Trust under the Confederate States.

5) The enumeration in the Constitution, of certain rights, shall not be construed to deny or disparage others retained by the people of the several States.

6) The powers not delegated to the Confederate States by the Constitution, nor prohibited by it to the States, are reserved to the States respectively, or to the people thereof.

ARTICLE VII

1) The Ratification of the Conventions of five States, shall be sufficient for the Establishment of this Constitution between the States so ratifying the same.

2) When five States shall have ratified this Constitution, in the manner before specified, the Congress under the Provisional Constitution shall prescribe the time for holding the election of President and Vice President; and for the meeting of the electoral college; and for counting the votes and inaugurating the President. They shall also prescribe the time for holding the first election of members of Congress under this Constitution, and the time for assembling the same. Until the assembling of such Congress, the Congress under the Provisional Constitution shall continue to exercise the legislative powers granted them, not extending beyond the time limited by the Constitution of the Provisional Government.

Adopted unanimously by the Congress of the Confederate States of South Carolina, Georgia, Florida, Alabama, Mississippi, Louisiana, and Texas, sitting in convention at the capitol, the city of Montgomery, Ala., on the eleventh day of March, in the year eighteen hundred and Sixty-one.

HOWELL COBB, President of the Congress.

South Carolina: R. Barnwell Rhett, C. G. Memminger, Wm. Porcher Miles, James Chesnut, Jr., R. W. Barnwell, William W. Boyce, Lawrence M. Keitt, T. J. Withers.

Georgia: Francis S. Bartow, Martin J. Crawford, Benjamin H. Hill, Thos. R. R. Cobb.

Florida: Jackson Morton, J. Patton Anderson, Jas. B. Owens.

Alabama: Richard W. Walker, Robt. H. Smith, Colin J. McRae, William P. Chilton, Stephen F. Hale, David P. Lewis, Tho. Fearn, Jno. Gill Shorter, J. L. M. Curry.

Mississippi: Alex. M. Clayton, James T. Harrison, William S. Barry, W. S. Wilson, Walker Brooke, W. P. Harris, J. A. P. Campbell.

Louisiana: Alex. de Clouet, C. M. Conrad, Duncan F. Kenner, Henry Marshall.

Texas: John Hemphill, Thomas N. Waul, John H. Reagan, Williamson S. Oldham, Louis T. Wigfall, John Gregg, William Beck Ochiltree.

www.ingramcontent.com/pod-product-compliance
Lightning Source LLC
Chambersburg PA
CBHW050337120526
44592CB00014B/2216